We Go to School

Sharon Coan, M.S.Ed.

then

now

then

now

then

now

ING GUIDE
FOUR FOOD GROUPS
Every day you need...
MILK
MEAT and EGGS
VEGETABLES and FRUITS
BREAD and CEREALS

then

now

then

now

then

Teacher Created Materials
search here
Look at the plum.
Where are the plums?

now

then

now

then

now

Write It!

1. Think about schools then.
2. Think about schools now.

3. Draw a picture of a school then.
4. Draw a picture of a school now.

Glossary

now—at the present time

then—in the past

Index

Your Turn!

How have schools changed? How are they the same? Tell about it.

Consultants

Shelley Scudder
Gifted Teacher
Broward County Schools

Caryn Williams, M.S.Ed.
Madison County Schools
Huntsville, AL

Publishing Credits

Conni Medina, M.A.Ed., *Managing Editor*
Lee Aucoin, *Creative Director*
Torrey Maloof, *Editor*
Lexa Hoang, *Designer*
Stephanie Reid, *Photo Editor*
Rachelle Cracchiolo, M.S.Ed., *Publisher*

Image Credits: Cover, p.1 Yellow Dog Productions/Getty Images; p.15 Bob Ebbesen/Alamy; p.17 H. Mark Weidman Photography/Alamy; p.5 Jim West/Alamy; p.22 Associated Press; p.2 H. Armstrong Roberts/Getty Images; p.23 Klaus Vedfelt/Getty Images; pp.8, 14 Post Archive/Getty Images; p.4 Time & Life Pictures/Getty Image; p.24 JoseGirarte/iStockphoto; p.9 Peter Zurek/iStockphoto; pp.6, 16 The Crowley Company/The Library of Congress; p.10 LOC [LC-USW3-000264-D]/The Library of Congress; p.12 Design Pics/Newscom; p.7 Stephanie Reid; pp.18–19 Teacher Created Materials; p.23 George Doyle/Thinkstock; All other images from Shutterstock.

Teacher Created Materials
5301 Oceanus Drive
Huntington Beach, CA 92649-1030
http://www.tcmpub.com

ISBN 978-1-4333-7339-8

Printed by 51250
PO 16654 / Printed in USA